Boats in the Attic

T0341549

POETS OUT LOUD

Elisabeth Frost, *series editor*

Boats in the Attic

Alison Powell

Fordham University Press   New York   2022

Fordham University Press has no responsibility for the persistence or accuracy of URLs for external or third-party Internet websites referred to in this publication and does not guarantee that any content on such websites is, or will remain, accurate or appropriate.

Fordham University Press also publishes its books in a variety of electronic formats. Some content that appears in print may not be available in electronic books.

Visit us online at www.fordhampress.com.

Library of Congress Control Number: 2017941386.

Printed in the United States of America

24 23 22   5 4 3 2 1

First edition

For my mother

Contents

Boats in the Attic

I

Missing File #1
Woolly Rhinoceros / Ancient Cavity Tooth

In 1930 a writer referred to the woolly rhinoceros as a monster, and its suffocation inside a tar pit as a sealing up in the oily earth. Bringing the big body to the earth was a challenge met by a young team of soldiers from the Polish Army. The giant horns had been used in ritual display; the soldiers noted drawings on the vertebrae by the man who killed it, or his sons, or his sons or daughters. The omission of garments and a ridiculous head are indications the Paleolithic artist possessed great skill. In poetry, exaggeration and elision are prized; also alliteration. Animals were more precisely drawn than humans, but this was not due to lack of ability. See for example Robin Hood Cave Horse. See for example Pin Hole Cave Man. Men drew themselves crudely, as if they had never seen one another or as though trapped alone in the oily earth or as if their eyes prevented them from seeing the human form as object. By contrast, they carved the animal likeness precisely, and in the animal's own bone. They crouched for warmth, taking on the hunched shape of a stone inside the cave where, later, their own unremarkable blank bones would be found. For a long time, drawings were carvings. For a long time, carvings were done on bone and art was a side effect of hunting.

An exciting development: as the large ice sheets of Siberia thaw, well-preserved remains of giant prehistoric monsters will reveal themselves. Let us hope the paleontologists are alert with their tools. When the water trickles out of the bath, the bright colored toys are scattered. I am already trying to clothe the child and warm the milk. I am "forward thinking," a "multi-tasker," a good worker. Now we do not need to call soldiers to lift the massive bodies, as we have sophisticated machines. We can lift the mammoth with only curiosity and propellers. Pin Hole Cave Man was found in 1928 by archaeologist A. L. Armstrong, who described the engraving as "a masked human figure in the act of dancing a ceremonial dance." He did not say why the figure was dancing, if he had just finished dinner, if he was making a house from bones, if he made the house for his children, who gathered; if the man, tired as he was from his hunting, worked late into the night, scraping the keratin from the bloody horn, presenting it to his daughter the next day as toy, as object of safety, sharp point, way to call for help.

The scientific name for the woolly rhino is Ancient Cavity Tooth, no, Coelodonta Antiquitatis, no, Commander in Chief, no, Stout, which means Extinct, which means Bog. The scientific name for the scientist is not Soldier, which means not Hunter but in between Scientist and Hunter. Like the soldiers who lifted the rhino to the earth and wrapped her in a receiving blanket and gifted her to the Polish Academy of Sciences. The scientist has no scientific name; in this he is like the Palaeolithic artist. Today a person goes by many names, official, gendered, mated, or otherwise.

The title of one article is "Siberia Surrenders Woolly Rhino Mysteries." It is not about the soldiers from Poland, who, having cracked the heavy body from the ice, carried it like one great watery mass walking in concert, humming a popular song. This is about another woolly rhino, "a female that was unearthed near the mouth of a Siberian gold mine," which sounds not more than vaguely sexual.

Yesterday Russia began air strikes against Syria. Siberia is not Russia, but it is not not Russia. The article's author did not mean Siberia as a nation-state. They meant the land: "Siberia is a major source of well-preserved remains, particularly as the long-frozen tundra surrenders carcasses as it thaws as a result of climate change."

Here the artist has made a place for you to encounter the woolly rhino. You may touch its nose. You may not feed it. It is a mummy; it has organs but they are sleeping. Here, please: _____

_____

_____

_____

_____

To surrender is a way to say to give oneself. To give oneself is a way to say one's self can be gifted, like the hollowed out horn. To compare land to a woman is a cliché of the highest order. It is laziness punishable only by the death of the poem. To say a poem is like a body is to say one's self is a machine. To say a body is erasable is to say extinction is a temperate clicking. And the howl is a hum, the wail a whirring.

These are the wrong things to say. These are pretty things to say. And like that, with one hand on the glass and one gloved hand inside the mouth of the woolly rhino, you have done it.

The First Word

of the Book of Revelation
is *apokalypsis*

       meaning *unveiling*

In the Book there is
great equality of number:

       twelve thousand of this tribe
       twelve thousand of that tribe

If one third of trees burned
one third of the ocean became blood

If one third of the sea creatures
died and floated to shore

then one third of the ships sank

       (equality but for the grass—
       the blades were comprehensively burned)

The sea draws in a breath of salt
revealing its floor—

       a flat labyrinth of bleached coral
       and divested wrecks—

and a red horse comes
expressly to take peace
from the earth

       during which one might hide
       with the children

or light a fire

and wait for someone
to come home

for good

Etymology: Heaven

Adam has a word for all—
even the beasts are given titles —

naming being the first form

       & knowing the weight of this
       & feeling himself

           become also
           light and hot as legend

Adam keeps a record

a list of words

       written in sap
       on animal bellies

       stretched on a loom of bones

until one day

       he rolls them
       tight as a motive

In Hebrew *heaven* is plural

       but is often translated
       into the singular

One is enough

One can encompass
the various notions of itself—

       is self-cleaning
       parthenogenetic

How the body

moves itself in
to the chimerical, the ideal—

       equinox, spinning egg
       a heart, a conveyor

       then an accountant

and at last

       the gates
       made of suddenness

The word *heaven*
comes from the suffix *-ham*

        not as in *pig*
        as in *to cover*

Many origins
are a type of covering—

        so that to come *from* somewhere
        is a way to clothe one's self

Maybe we came from heaven
and will return to it

        as if heaven was a yolk
        cupped inside us

Anyway we are distracted

        we've made up a feast
        to absorb our mouths and hands—

        fearing, as we do,
        idleness and playthings

All living things are godsent
All things living will be used

It is right to be skeptical
but think

how sensible he was

to take the heaven
of first names—

        the story of religion
        he had begun alone

                without helpmeet—

and record it

        on the elastic borderland
        of a body

to see

        how slippery
        naming becomes

The Great Disappointment, 1844

A girl from out West packed a trunk

        silk chintz   petticoats   calfskin boots

wound it with leather straps
and sat upon it like a soldier

waited for the Rapture
like waiting to be asked   to dance

Wouldn't you wish
to bring with you

        the things that make you   love yourself

What a simple thing
to mistake
           day to mean *year*

as a child might exchange

           on and *off*
           light for *dark*

knowing only that both
are matters of degree

Reverend Miller gathered thousands

        they swaddled themselves
        in white Ascension Robes

he instructed them to curl inside

their metal washtubs
up on the hill

Under the white circle of tents
chests full of anticipation

      a steady flood of saliva
      as when   having been starved

      one waits for meat

Miller wrote:

> *The right equation will come   from the clouds of heaven*
> *The numbers possess us*
>
> *The body of every departed numeral*
> *will be raised and destroy wicked error*

During this time
he developed a tremor

a skin condition
transformed his skin
to a thick dimpled peel

> so he was in appearance
> more devil than prophet

As ever

homecomings are unsure
and heavy

> *Let the correct sum of the earth*
> *meet us*
> *as equations in the air*

Missing File #2
A Few Facts about Bees

Bees have two stomachs: one for eating, one for storage. They suffer from "disappearing disease." Bees have undertakers who carry the dead and dying away from the hive. A single worker bee makes 1/12 a teaspoon of honey in his lifetime. In April a truck carrying hundreds of hives as freight glanced off a guardrail, flipped, and released fourteen million bees to the air. It had been traveling through America's wettest city to a local blueberry farm, which the honeybees were to pollinate for pennies on the dollar.

When I was a child, I licked manuka honey off the spoon when sick. I yanked handfuls of honeysuckle from the neighbor's vine. I would pull the pistil out of the flower carefully to release what I had been told was honey.

The vines covered a neighbor's fence; a woman lived there with six exotic birds and a pale withdrawn daughter. Together the girl and I would collect horse apples in the front yard and examine them carefully for caterpillars. We'd return at dusk to her house, which had one room just for the birds, branches anchored to the windows and extending all around.

"Disappearing disease" sounds psychological or cultural in nature, as if the bees, having come from ancient Egypt, watched Western modernity collapse and returned to the pyramids. When the truck turned the bees loose they scrambled, trying to find position, to signal the way like a compass. The driver wrapped his arms over his face, and local reporters were stung until clusters of the bodies of bees littered the interstate.

When faced with a predator, bees do the Wave: they flick their clear wings, arch their bodies, and send a ripple across the comb. Like this, a queen is protected all winter: the workers huddle around her, quivering to keep the heat up. They rotate from the outer to inner ring so no one is left long out in the cold. Her whole life the workers feed her, bowing to release royal jelly from the glands in their heads.

The neighbor's red-nosed, jovial husband had a diminutive nickname and drove a truck for a living. He hung himself in the basement many years later, to everyone's surprise.

The bees swarm into the boxes. We organize the boxes and send them into the gasoline atmosphere; the bees are then released to do their tremble dances in the cool mist of an automatic sprinkler. But transportation is not predation. Is it.

The First Deluge: A Found Poem

on the question of space in Noah's Ark   according to
Noah's Ark: A Feasibility Study   the vast   majority
of species   could survive in water   jelly fish   and
hydroids 5,000 species of sponges worms   very large animals
the dinosaur or elephant would be represented by young ones
Furthermore the word *specie*   is not equivalent to   *created
kinds* in Genesis   in which there were as few as two thousand
animals   The ark could accommodate   sixteen thousand
padding this number   for error   still you see it is a matter
of language   before it is a matter of mathematics Assume the
average animal to be the size   of a sheep there would have
been ample space   to carry the animals filling just 37% of the
ark   plenty of room for food and baggage   plus Noah's
family of eight people

              The Ark had plenty   of space
the bigger problem   would have been   the construction
but the Bible indicates Noah did this   under   divine
guidance and there is no reason to believe   he did not hire
additional workmen   The door   to the ark was closed
God destroyed the world   you see   it is a matter of
_____ before it is a matter of _____

Mrs. Noah: A Found Poem

(incidentally contrary to popular opinion   Mrs.   Noah   would
have been far from primitive   Mrs. Noah was not a nobody
she faithfully helped Noah   nothing but sheer steel could
have weathered the cries   of those drowning   great
grace   must have been granted her to be shut in   with many
thousands of animals   for more than a year   on   their
enormous houseboat   three sons hammering in her ears   of
the coming doom   Noah responsible   he the one called to
account when they   disobeyed God   I think that Mrs.
Noah   would not have had a problem with this   even though
she started it)

Missing File #3
Panthera Leo Leo, Or, A Civics Lesson

A girl walks down the hallway in junior high wearing stone-washed jeans and a choker, assuming no one will touch her though many will look. As Aristotle writes *The lion . . . progress[es] by an amble; the action so called is when the animal never overpasses the right with the left but always follows close upon it.* This may appear artful but isn't, as a cat traverses the sill of an open window. The middle school has no walls, just folding accordion slats to divide classrooms into four blocks—*genera*—named for the colors of the school and its mascot. Gold Block. Black Block. The girl imagines her body losing a dimension, her self a pocket door; a way to evade the predatory place altogether.

Aristotle's *History of Animals* is thorough; at times it is accidentally funny, as when he writes *Hedgehogs copulate erect, belly to belly* or that lions don't have under-eyelashes and piss backwards. Other times Aristotle states the obvious—e.g., *Furthermore, of animals some are horned and some are not so.* Is he being hubristic, believing his account will survive the extinction of the thing itself, thinking he records because he is the only one to see? Or is he being pessimistic, assuming the horned / unhorned animals are temporary and therefore necessitate description? Like this, the banal is transformed by annihilation into the marvelous.

Most likely Aristotle's tone reveals affectation of style, not spirit. Or he was simply so entranced with the act of describing that readers are swept out into the sea of his mind, as when a magician sweeps the tablecloth off the table, leaving behind a centerpiece still in place.

Spring afternoons, 1993, the yellow buses line the cul-de-sac looking mean-spirited and institutional. White dogwood blooms shed onto the steps at the school entrance. I hate them: the moment they bloom, the boys start joking that they smell *just like pussy.*

That spring a girl has a seizure in our biology class, thrashes about on the floor like a fish on the speckled deck of a boat. The teacher kneels down and removes the girl's shoes, inexplicably. We'd been reading an article about extinction; the teacher, projecting images onto the gray cinderblock wall, had explained it as a process nearly done and nearly undone, many times over. *The last wild Atlas lion was killed by a French colonial hunter in 1922 in Morocco on Atlas mountain— that is, a mountain bearing the lion's own name.* Cut to grainy shot of a heavy lion head, gripped by the mane by a smiling man with the requisite wide stance. The author added with anemic wit: *The history books may have left a chapter or two out of the story.*

Later that day one of the boys—maybe emboldened by the sight of the epileptic girl in that moment of biological abandon—grabs my friend by the dogwood and shoves her against a wall. He bares his teeth at her, says *Ooh. Ooh I like that.*

Extinction is a very old book, sliced open and re-sealed over and over. In writing a report on extinction, one must note the multiple names used for a single species: for instance, the Atlas lion may also be called the Barbary lion, Moroccan Royal lion, or *Panthera leo leo*. You must record the killings of all three to know whether the species is truly a goner.

Extinction is a symphony of killings in different time signatures. In the Roman Empire, the state imported Barbary lions from North Africa for gladiator games; also for baiting, where a lion battles a pack of dogs while encircled by drunk human spectators. Lion baiting was a blood sport with a long run: King James I of England kept his lions in the Tower, a floor above the traitors and heretics, because it was fun to watch lions tear apart dogs like toys—at least as fun as sitting around identifying witches, his other pastime. Yet he let his polar bear amble into the Thames on a long silver chain to hunt for fish all on its own.

Sometimes I think of naming as a paternal act: Adam sits, petting the animals as they come to him, making of them the first little zoo. Other times I think naming is a symbol of anxiety— if we don't have a word for something, maybe it won't let us hold it anymore.

Journalism, fourth period. I sit at my green melamine desk and record the objects in the room: "The yellow ribbed border paper is torn slightly in the left corner. Below it is a faint chalk mark, roughly an inch in length," etc. I do not write about Shelley, with her satin jacket, skunk mane of black hair, and thin black eyeliner, who has threatened to beat my ass at the trailer park across the street after school any day now. I do not write about the baseball-hat-wearing Christian girl who was my science partner and who recently shot herself. I do not write that I think it was because she loved girls or wanted to be a boy or both, I'm not sure. Nor do I write about the pockmarked Civics teacher who invites me to sit on his lap or to swim with him after school and counts aloud the days until his retirement at the start of each class.

Anyhow, description does not involve, but is itself, a type of movement. The movement can be of an accidental or strategic kind; most often it is a combination, as when one jokes about their childhood while a little bit drunk at a party. More naming means more strategy, more accidents, more baiting. *Gold Block. Science Partner.*

I wonder where Shelley is now. She lives in my brain and sparkles with her violence.

Critical Thinking, first period. We sit for a fifty-minute class in an open square space with almond-colored plastic accordion walls. I sit near my friend who has gap-teeth and reddish blond hair that makes her look a little wild though she's no lion, just a breeze.

The teacher—male, early thirties—makes frequent use of an overhead projector. In a lesson on criteria, he uses a special red pen to outline qualities of the Perfect Woman: *a) green eyes b) blond hair* and *c) a curvaceous body weighing appx. 105 to 110 pounds.* I know what *curvaceous* means but some don't, so he adds in red marker *Big Breasts, Backside*, then has us look it up in a dictionary anyway. Finally, he demonstrates the limitations of criteria in critical thinking by explaining how a curvaceous waitress infected him with a painful sexually transmitted disease.

With these examples, he uses his hands to wrap up us girls and place us outside the beige slatted city walls. We know what is happening. We wait there by the gate, looking at our clawed feet.

Aristotle says, *Many animals have memory, and are capable of instruction; but no other creature except man can recall the past at will.* Aristotle says:

A) *Man is by nature a political animal.*
B) *What separates humans from animals is rationality.*
C) *The city is a machine.*
D) *Machine.*

Aristotle says the city is organic, which is like saying cruelty is organic. Or rather, it is like saying division of resources and power is organic, which is like saying cruelty is organic.

Erasing takes a long time: the rain of pink rubber shreds, the rubbery smell of it. The girl writes in her notebook: *Miss Royal Leo, Leo Royal Atlas,* drawing a lion with hearts for eyes, listing her favorite things about lions and gladiators.

She has been here a long time. Her position continues to be imperfect.

The Other, The Other

She carries many things,
children, etc., so Adam holds
the door, Adam who stretches
from earth to heaven wearing
the rough cape of a carapace.
This is the time before time,
you know, before cause and effect,
and by *children* I mean bushels
and bushels of bounty.
For who can resist Adam.
Especially way back when
one ocean was one eye, the other,
the other, and the heel of his foot
so bewildering in its beauty
it for real blocked the sun.
By beginning with the woman
I'm telling this story wicked
backwards. The conch shell
was shaped like an ear
in homage for what Adam
heard, himself and the language
he made up, just coming
from him like the erotic before
the other more sticky erotic,
what's more sexy than *lizard*
and *poppy, hawk,* really, coming
up with all of it on your own,
the only one, the original.
For a time, Adam was thought
to have been Janus-faced,
split, sewn back to back
and separated like a decal,
kind of like the outline

a woman can become by carrying
so many things, children, etc.
They said he made the desert
by scraping his heel against
Eve's cheek, leaving the impression
of a land made only of cacti
traversed at night by wolves.
Until it all broke apart.
Point is, because this story
turns into the story of truth,
I'm afraid you'll laugh at me
if I try to make up another,
less punitive story,
one where our first mother
and father aren't punished
for exploding like stars
but are instead allowed to float
in the blackness of their own making,
together in the subzero amniotic stardust
listening to the Modern Lovers—
anything but Adam and Eve
eating altars made of their own hunger
before turning to each other
at the same time yelling

> *What are you doing*
> *Who do you take me for*

In the Beginning

you know that saying *in the beginning was the word* well the
word   is too pleased with itself *liberty* say or *personhood*
running up and down along the garden fence trailing streamers
behind it   while we shout   *You can't run like this*   as
though it is   a bolting child   I mean the word   has never
been what we supposed it to be   To be honest   the   word
hates our guts   We worked it into a nub so it grew wings & a
little twin engine   & now it's always moving   when it
knows full well we need it not to move   I   can't
shake the feeling—   if only the word loved us   didn't
treat us like the dumb kid   on the school bus who likes magic
Now that we're big enough   to hate   the word right back
we pluck at it   *the word loves me   the word loves me not*
loose lips sink ships   *Sally's lips sink ships*   but the word
is swollen with blood   you know it never had any truck with
love   These days it just lies down in its cage   next to
plastic tubing &   turns its shaved body   away from us

II

If We Speak of the Hurricane

of whiteness and the horn of plenty,
if it is even a horn; if there is such a thing
if destruction is ceaseless; if my son's hand
reaches for a cotton blanket or a cat's tail,
if we have our eyes on him, if I describe
his hand as *pillowy*; if the world is a tower
of breakable plates for the white son,
if he is unaware of the supernatural-seeming
inventions that sustain white hunger;
if Hades has its own horn made of ivory
for drinking; if hunger tightens the guts
of others; if it is described as *inevitable*
or *accidental*; if the description is written
by the same hunger; if he is just a boy
asking about justice at the mall;
if his father and I cannot help but love
his locomotive of curiosity, its erratic perpetuity,
shark, shots, Mars, if we wonder how it will end;
if zoo doctor, if astronomer, if madman;
if we speak of the white shark, if they are
nearly missing, if the bleaching of coral;
if the four of us trudge upstairs at bedtime
single file making train sounds are we acting
as a tribe; if we fear the world; if four feels a tribe;
if our son assigns himself the role of conductor;
if his sister laughs, cheek against my shoulder;
if I carry her body carefully like her body were glass,
a white object; if tired from school, my son dreams
of cities lit up and falling, fireflies collapsing,
bees and honey; if at school he traces letters
with happy concentration; if, using a push pin
to punch out the shapes of continents he asks
his teacher why he cannot punch out the ocean,

why just continents, why can't he pin-punch the ocean;
if at school he pours water from a red pitcher
into a bowl, spills some, threads yarn through a card;
if twice yearly there is the interruption
of a lockdown drill, the crackling loudspeaker,
if his teacher asks anyone who is afraid
to raise their hand, if she says

> *This is for the wild animal*
> *who may at any moment enter*

After the Birth of the First Child

Eyelids like Elizabethan opera house stage curtains. Belly worrier.
You took the silver streak from Brooklyn and came to us, a bright
blue level eight zipline capillary. When the first storm came and
filled the tunnels with locusts your father and I gave the one boat
to you, our tongue tied boy. Together we ran from room to room
in the tenement house. What were we looking for? You feasted on
wheels and ovals while we waited in the dacha playing ping pong
with our half shadows. We didn't recognize the other, were light
up bouncing balls hurled by a bear. I was a clump of hair, I was
in stitches, a peacock picking its way over the icy fountain. Now
I am a shepherd and your father is a shepherd and we guard you,
the small hurricane that whirls from room to room. You burrower
of the yellow kitchen. You hard working moth. Bicycling tragedy
maestro, ingenue, hyacinth. Samson offering honey from the
lion's body. Matryoshka of forgiveness. It is winter. We are
dragons. I am also a baker. I keep forgetting what kind of mother
I am but you don't mind.

The Book of Revelation

Someone has given my mother a white robe
in the waiting room of the hospital

and has told her to wait
until I am through it

Inside the suite   I recall

       having once seen

       the black x-ray of a horse
       the gray smoke of its movement

       head turned to look
       impossibly behind itself

       the barrel rib cage

the heart

       a wide sunflower
       heavy as a bell

The time comes   when the earth
is that heavy

     the moon

     separated from its host
     begins to recoil and spin
     in the brightness

a fray into which

     someone has piled
     an eternity of black hair

Mine—

     I was a girl

my mother gave me
warm figs for dessert
and read from a book

     An island is part of the earth

     its existence
     a kind of breech

     into the hands of the day

For just a few minutes now
I am still a child

I picture the x-ray

       my mother in the other room
       alone
              nothing underfoot

Then he is born
       placed upon me

uncanny eyes
       like my eyes

an open mouth

This writes over
the child I was

briskly

       as a dressmaker
       undresses someone
       for a fitting

Like this
the first child arrived

as through the ocean's
oily gates

Then came closing time—
a paper bed made of worry

and waking,
no sleep

      (*deprive* a word that can mean
      removed from ecclesiastical office

      so removed from the heaven
      of one's right mind)

I cannot remember
my body without vertigo

or what it felt   to feel

      anything other than animal

In the parking lot of Home Depot
a middle-aged man puts his head
on a steering wheel

His young daughter
listens to top 40 radio
in the backseat

I think

>   Not so bad to lose
>   with the earth
>   those terrible lyrics—

>>   *I'm in love with the shape of you*
>>   *We push and pull like a magnet do*

I start to play a game—

I imagine everything
disappearing all at once

kind of like synching a phone

>   boll weevils   respirators
>   war memorials   debt
>   spoons   dandelions
>   pigeons   gunshots
>   formaldehyde   errands

>   every sneering corsage

Red lights flash under the debris

Now that I am a mother
I almost never dream

but when I do
I'm sorry

                  I dream of apocalypse

At the YMCA
children wait
for their turn to swim

and pass the time

slapping the water
making up games

     and taunts

       I am a shark
       I am a rainbow dolphin

       I am going to eat your eyes
       I am going to eat your world

Finally it's my son's turn

He dives into the water

       I wave in the air
       a toy wooden dog on wheels

       he has asked me to bring
       to make sure it sees

When he was about two
he'd mix up words

       say *missing*
       when he meant *loving*

clutching the dog
to his chest

looking down at it
saying in his soft voice

    Missing

One day in the car
our son, now four, says

What's funny about the sun Mama
is that the sun is a star
we only see in the daytime

Trying to sort it out
he elongates his syllables

flattens his palm
and slices the air   like a warrior

He goes on like this for days—

magic planets made of gas

stars collapsing
in on themselves

the uneven universe
like a house without walls

Then riddles of time and space—

that if you take infant twins
and separate them

housing one at sea level
and another atop a mountain

then reunite them late in life
they will discover

one is now older   than the other

At the pet store
he watches tanks of goldfish

the paper-thin fins
flit back and forth

     a little festival of sequins

He *really really* wants one

For luck   he says

     his voice curatorial
     a little aggrieved

He doesn't remember
the red betta we had

when we still lived
in the city where he was born

For years it looped around
two sticks of bamboo

in a round house

     and he would watch it
     and knew its name—

       Lucky, as it happens

At the nursery he chooses
two kinds of bulbs to plant

and appraises them daily

Like this he begins

        cultivating the earth
        as though he has nothing   but time

One afternoon he stands at the sink
washing hands

        red hair in the bright light

The next he leaves us
for the city

        or has some place he has to go

What I mean is

where does the child
playing house

        in a clearing of mind

               begin and end   and begin

One day I am back
in the modern hospital

costumed as it is
like a nice hotel—

little soaps shaped like leaves
and piped music

as though I could forget where I am, what I must do

We've gone ahead and done it—
another child coming

despite the earth
in face of everything

an act of foolish decisiveness

like teenagers at night
in the woods

who have taken off
everything

It is time—

a spotlight descends

from a hidden panel
in the ceiling

Our daughter
born easily

is not even five pounds

      but her eyelashes darken daily
      and the fontanelle pulses

She grows in a steady   sure way

      unlike the blackworm
      that splits and regenerates

      eight heads
      to aerate the earth

      making eight new rooms within it

In the front yard—   spring—

       gnats orbit a bowl
       of half consumed fruit

My newborn daughter
opens and closes her mouth

       like a fish

We see a hyacinth
has finally appeared—

at the tight blue comb of bloom
my son narrows his eyes

           rips it from its stem

           and pushes the petals
           into his mouth

Like this

       curiosity and good cheer
       are cousin to greed

This is where
the temples of faith
are built
          and rebuilt

From then on
it seems

       he talks
       like a child king

Maybe the man
digging into the velvet sack
of the ocean floor

      isn't a devil

We want everything
don't we

      mouths full of crushed petals

      one child   then another

Athena with her goatskin shield
fringed in snakes

      her head of Medusa

Maybe the story of destruction
is also the story of salvation

      like a door that swings

You may make your own—
many have before you—

      from,   say

      bird bone and gorilla palm
      tusk and hot hinges

      earth core   and more tusk

Our daughter
has just begun to talk

she sings alone to herself
in her room

like the butterfly

      half in   half out
      of the pupa

waiting for its wings to dry

      to understand
      what it is now capable of

Remember   curious Alice

      the box, the small cake
      studded with currants

How she shrinks
then grows

      then shrinks again

in her dizzy mannered cocoon

From reading the Book
I learn it is never a good sign

when   opening a book

a white horse gallops from it
having been kicked hard

            by a man in the shadows

Then a red horse comes
expressly to take your peace
from you

The man riding it

wants to starve and throw
a quarter of your people

            to beasts

In one dream
I am not sure who I am

but I know
the pale horse

            pale as an x-ray
            comes next

so I hide behind the door

            below the bed
            is an encyclopedia of lost things

My son loves dinosaurs

loves them no less
for being gone forever

      has been told
      about what happened

      and what will

We begin to consider
other planets

      Would they have us?

First the planet the ancients saw
as the god of thunder

      which is in fact belted by clouds
      and hosts an interminable storm

Then the one Emerson could see
with his translucent eyeball

      though not its hundred and fifty
      frozen moons

Finally the one upon which
we most long to dwell

      the one made of iron and arithmetic
      the one the color of blood

         that ovals the sun
         in warlike redundancy

Summer in the backyard
they make wishes
on white dandelion threads

we pretend
we're unknown creatures

on some unpopulated
indestructible island

They wave a telescope

       expand   collapse
       expand   collapse

There is no top to it

       they shout

meaning the sky

Everything says to them—
they say to me all the time—

     DRINK ME

He that has an ear
let him hear it

      I would fasten their small hearts
      to my heart with reins

For now   let me watch

as their bones
slowly inch forth

entrepreneurial

      as a farmer
      or a new religion

Upon Turning Forty

I am trying not to sleep here   trying not to be a child performing
an etude in tight shoes forever   I adopt an attitude   a
little Italian greyhound   named Baby I live   inside two
lit windows and a gray horse   near that parking
lot in Williamsburg & the ice cream truck though the market
is   overall   a place of global sadnesses shell
necklaces shell mobiles   I was once maybe the second
life   of the party   the bees wings   once I conquered
the blackjack table   sang   until my blood broke   and my
own grandfather   even the watermelon sank   like a cake
in a cupboard   it was remarkable   it was there
the whole time   yet didn't attract bugs   the fruit stayed
delicious   now sailing on in a sandstorm   I am my
own tongue trying to stay in my mouth   it's embarrassing
when I catch myself   on the street   in August looking
eager   it's Saturday night   talk to me   I am a you
who could be anyone   lined   like an atlas a hand
made of graphite   to do your writing with a volunteer
opportunity with the local hospital   stay

Missing File #4
Already We Are Less than Ever Before

Fereidoun M. Esfandiary, transhumanist philosopher and champion of cryonics, hypothesized the sun was the heart of utopia. He changed his name to FM-2030 to mark the year he'd turn 100. Interviewed by Larry King, FM-2030 wears a heavy white robe and says his new name is "neat." Larry smiles indulgently. "Do you believe people will be named this way in the future?" FM-2030 says "No. We will have the ability to change season. 2030 will be a magical time, a dream, a goal: we will be ageless. Everyone will have an excellent chance to live forever." FM-2030 must have felt especially disappointed when dying of pancreatic cancer so early, at 69. As for the sun— bountiful with free energy, FM-2030 said it would run machines, copy everything and ourselves, so we'd never run out of anything ever again. No more competition. We'd stop beating up on each other. Plus, synthetic organs would make death a relic. *Why swell'st thou? Death, thou shalt die*, etc. Larry King is fixated on the name, like a big gray bear hunched over a ball. "You are not saying by taking this name that we will be named this way. But we will have our heritage," Larry goes on, straightening his tie. "Already we are less hereditarian than ever before," replies FM-2030 in a subdued, heroic way.

Elsewhere FM-2030 said, "I am a 21st century person accidentally launched in the 20th. I have a deep nostalgia for the future." He said the pancreas is a stupid, dumb, wretched organ. More than 100 people have been cryopreserved since 1967, housed in metal cylinders full of liquid nitrogen in a warehouse. When a body is preserved—not just a brain—the patient is a "whole body member." With his new name, FM-2030 demonstrates how renaming is a form of discovery, the apprehension of a new identity or use for an existing thing. It's marvelous how a tongue, making a sound received by the ear, transforms in the mind a material, giving it a use well beyond its present existence. You know what I mean? Just, wow.

Lately my son talks a lot about Getting Dead: "Actually I don't like this flavor lip balm. I'm giving it to you, to have for your whole life until you get dead!" At bedtime: "What was I going to ask? Oh. What happens when your life is done?" The books say: Offer nothing beyond the scope of the child's question. As if that's possible, as if every call and response weren't a widening circle. In *The Prelude,* Wordsworth writes of a boy standing on a cliff, imitating the owls who respond in kind until the mountain and pool below become a mess of sounds, a tornado in-a-bottle: the owl call, the hollow echo of the boy's call, render indistinguishable what is human or animal, echo or utterance. Or even what speech is anyhow. Wordsworth offers a metaphor: the idea of origin is the naivest—or possibly vainest—of human concepts.

When I was a child, a friend with straw-like hair and the body of a translucent scarecrow told me how her aunt, a farmhand, died by falling into a silo. Echo. Echo. Echo.

A twenty-something woman tells her Reddit followers she has terminal cancer and asks for donations. The funds aren't for a cure, but to have her brain cryopreserved after death. She succeeds, though not enough to be a whole body member. Now her father records daily messages for her future/afterlife brain. They all begin the same: "Hello, honey…"

Incidentally, Mormons don't believe people get a planet populated with their own families after death, but they don't exactly refute it. If that were true my mother, father, brother, and I would end up on our own planet with my mother's cousin, Mary, a severe anorexic from the backwoods who once tried to kill her own mother by throwing piece after piece of hot fried chicken at her in a rage.

The Reddit girl was engaged; her fiancé wondered if he should be frozen, too, eternally bound to his extraordinary ice girl in her super form. Today he is married to an organic woman and works for a conservative think tank.

Wordsworth's owls never appear to us or the boy. It's unclear whether the event—the eruption—happens at sundown, or sunset. The poet leaves it ambiguous. Determining what is the midpoint of day or night is a fool's errand anyway. What is clear is that the boy dies, ending up at the bottom of the lake below a shimmery surface reflecting the sky and *that uncertain heaven.*

Once I took my son to AquaTots Swim Club and tried to make him into a Goldfish. We circled together in the water while a big man we didn't know shouted at us enthusiastically, instructing me to dunk my son's head underwater and I did it because I thought it was good for him. What did I know. He emerged full of newfound courage, but when we left he was clutching a purple plastic dolphin that lights up underwater, begging never to return.

When I turn 40, my son gives me a card shaped like Frida Kahlo and says "It's Daylight Savings Time, you have a choice: you can turn either 11 or dead!" That night I see Patti Smith perform live with my Mormon friend Lisa. Patti shakes her hips and shoots the stink eye at anyone recording with an iPhone; Lisa and I toast our mules to *Horses*.

As a kid, just reading the word *death* made my stomach flip-flop: the actual letters and my somatic recoil became nearly indistinguishable from its meaning. The *d* was the worst but the way *-eath* follows like a slack, wet sheet felt terrible and viral. Now a mother, I imagine a children's book titled *Breaking the Bad News*. Table of Contents: Death: subsection, Cancer. Things That Eat People: Sharks, Bears, Other People. Capitalist Fictions: Linear Progress, Heaven. One day, after saying something so full of grace the words hang in the air as if made of filament, wisdom, and sugar, you'll trip over an electrical wire or something and fall flat on your face. You're an animal, not a god. 39 is not one of your choices.

Are you ready? I believe you are ready.

III

Missing File #5
The Ortolan Bunting

In 1996, former French President François Mitterand invited thirty guests to his last supper. One was delighted to attend and offer condolences, admittedly a delicate balancing act. President Mitterand sat mute at the head of the table, blankets wound around him, eyes glorious and blank as bicycle reflectors. In the corners were his bodyguards. At first he seemed to be sleeping, but with a sweeping blur of white linen— when the servants arrived with *the birdies*, the chef called them—the former President grinned, teeth shined in spit. The size of the birds was delightful, as if the very soul of France had been draped across a fig. A tiny dog no more efficiently arouses sympathy.

The thirty guests and the dying President assumed what is called the "eating posture," draping napkins over their heads like brides or nuns, so as not to offend God for masticating the soul of France. At last spooning the birds into their mouths, biting into thirty hazelnut heads, the guests agreed it would have been a shame to waste what had been bound and drowned in Cognac. (I would have peeked through my napkin.) The President died seven days later having refused subsequent food, stuffed to the end with two small winged souls of France. The media was unrelenting. *Two!*

Some ornithologists translate birdsong into human language: to assist with memory, perhaps, or feel they've bridged a divide or to make jokes. For example, the ortolan song is known as *A little bit of bread and no cheese* which sounds like a child rhyme, mice running from the carving knife, and makes me think of a dumbshow, because you could mime, easily, *A little bit of bread*, and even *no cheese,* the dissatisfaction with one's plate by waving your hands with a furrowed brow and exaggerated frown.

Ortolan eggs are pearly and covered in veins, and the real song of the ortolan is here written, but that song is not a phrase but a series of ridiculous words. The ortolan nest is a kind of bowl made of horsehair and *noisome weeds*, according to John Clare, the great poet of bird nests and being poor. Inside the bowl the eggs are sly, holding the pattern for next and next ortolans.

I know one ornithologist who has the singing voice of a sexless ghost continent. Once I write to ask about the bird in *The Progress of Ryhme*. What is it? I ask. I have been comparing the birdsong in the poem to a mirror stage, where the poet sees how separate he is from the bird. His mastery sounds like this: *Wew-wew wew-wew, chur-chur chur-chur Woo-it woo-it … Tee-rew tee-rew tee-rew tee-rew Chew-rit chew-rit Will-will will-will grig-grig grig-grig.* The ornithologists writes back: a nightingale. I believe him to be weary of citizens and their ignorance of birds.

The Mitterand affair increases the ortolan's value among poets. Everywhere I look there is another poem for the ortolan: behind the checkout counter at the deli, inside the mailbox, inside the cherry wood dresser of America's guilt. I myself have never understood the love of birds, which refuse to be held. Of the proliferation of ortolan poems, I worry. How will I sell my own poem on the ortolan? I feel betrayed by the little victims shut up in a box, by their magnetic needle bones. I begin to sympathize with the eater.

Maybe it's not to want to be God to use what God gave you, not sinister nor hubristic to place the body in your mouth and pierce the head with your front teeth like a stapler. Surely deliciousness is not a thing your mother gives you before slapping you for what you are, a little beast made of hunger and curiosity. It is so like you— to forget what you are, just like an animal. Maybe the bird was a gray seducer of kings and emperors. Shut up in the box in the dark, consuming all the figs without stopping until the sticky seeds lined its intestines like diamonds. What if it doesn't see the dark bath coming but still accepts it, even loves it a little, its cage a little Moses basket. *Grig-grig.* What if that.

Missing File #6
Horns-a-Plenty

Narrow the human eye on the rare thing, and it tends toward disappearance. We take a special tooth and preserve it in Vaseline, then sell it or wear it. The closet full of furs. The lock of hair cut and put in a book, braided into a wedding ring. If it has horns we pull the horns from it and drill screws into it. The gate of a ranch in Ely, Nevada is made of the six, eight, ten point antlers of bucks. It stands mute and unwilling against the blue desert sky, a puzzle made of bleached coral or the gates of some weird amusement park. This is the West.

Until she died, my great-grandmother Safrona prized a paperweight, a smooth dome the size of an infant fist. Inside it was a scorpion arrested in resin, pedipalps hinged open. Below the bed she kept other things, seen and unseen: a shotgun shell from a military funeral, an envelope with the hair of her infant son, long dead. Peacock feet. Her twin sister Sarona. Bilocation, bird's nest soup, the flower called Life within Death—its brown netted globe that encircles the red fruit.

I like my words rare, syllables whittled into slivers of hymn. A group of crows makes a murder, but murder is a word and so for the crow a thing unspeakable. Lucky for us, the Tower of Babel is an all-you-can-eat-buffet. Outside, the pruned deer secrete in the wilderness.

Conditions

Animals drift out there
in the monotonous green

      of Chernobyl

A fact known to most of us
theoretically

      which is to say
      photographically

Wolves using the magnetic fields
of the earth to find their way

      developing a cryptography
      for the centuries

      to which we are not invited

I like to think of the wolf, the boar
as parentheticals

    littering a final corner
    of this intestinal kingdom

but I know we are the curved bracket

    the sea waiting to gulp
    our world of metal

    down like an oyster

and the heat

    having waylaid the ice
    wrapping a plush robe of steam

    around us

leading us to the edge
of everything

Bless us, then

— having actually written the thing
and written it again

       and laid it out before us—

our astonishment

eyes skyward
open mouths

       little drowned fowl

Together, let us memorize

the red carpet
rice thrown at weddings
the ark on the mountaintop

how we had gripped
the wheel

       like a god
       inflammable

No one believed the boy

not because there was
an absence
of wolves

but because no one trusts
a psychoneurotic

       oh but the little footprints
       each small cry—Wolf!—

       made in the boy heart
       what about the sheep heart

       the metaphor heart
       what

Boats in the Attic

It had been so dry. Wildfires
blooming into a continent of ash.
Papers, chronicles of hopeless
arbitration, swept the sidewalk.

On the shifting wrack line,
sea anemones scattered
their neon orange tentacles
like streamers.

Elephants paraded into the city
and their tusks seemed to us
not like parentheses
of our time on earth, but like

shadeless boats, or huge,
simple grins of yellow bone.
A tailor unpinned the clothes
from a mannequin he'd known

so well it seemed a shadow
of the family he'd always wanted.
In the end, daughter, it was
the thing that was called for

years *holy*. You and me,
sitting criss-cross applesauce,
pretending to row
all the way to shore.

Missing File #7
Nomen Nudum

Had they made as good provision for their names as they
have done for their relics, they had not so grossly erred in
the art of perpetuation. But to subsist in bones, and be but
pyramidally extant, is a fallacy in duration.

— Sir Thomas Browne

Geologist Rev. William Buckland (1784–1856), of the Society
for the Acclimatization of Animals, distinguished professor of
Oxford University, spent his free time eating his way through
the animal kingdom. Believing the stomach ruled the world
because it could eat the world, he consumed sea slugs, earwigs,
kangaroo, seal, porpoise, dog, and more. His voracious appetite
was an inspiration: acquaintance John Ruskin— botanist,
watercolorist— lamented missing one of Buckland's favorite
snacks of grilled mice on toast.

I feel close to him, and want you to as well. From here on let us
call him William. At a dinner party in 1848, William and his
fellow guests were shown what appeared to be a pumice stone in
a silver casket, only to learn it was the relic heart of Louis XIV of
France, taken from the royal tomb by a scorned member of the
family. The guests were the last to see it, for William announced
*I have eaten many strange things, but I have never eaten the heart of
a king!* before gobbling it up like so much dried jerky.

Will was a geologist, but he was also a priest; perhaps the gesture
was accompanied by a loosening of the clerical collar. This gives
the scene an even more obviously subversive flair. Had William
resisted eating the king's heart he could have studied it. Perhaps
gulping it down was a way to say, *knowledge is less than hunger.
History is less than experience. Monarchy is less than death.*

One article about William reads: *he voraciously consumed knowledge as if it were the bread of life.* This is a simile made of two metaphors; it is redundant, as eating is redundant.

My first love and I once drove from Indiana to a cabin in Vermont, where we met a philosopher who said if, instead of eating, there was a pill to take that would provide all nutrients necessary to live, he'd be the first to sign up. In his spare time, the philosopher sang country ballads with the voice of George Jones, and I desired him very much, though his lack of passion for gastronomy and seeming asexuality were surely related. Also I was painfully in love with his good friend. Too much appetite, I guess. I think of the pill he says he'd take. I imagine it must be unlike any other pill in the world. Perhaps it could be shaped to look like food: a miniature egg, say, or a tiny apple.

A philosopher is unlike a geologist in important ways. If a geologist is an explorer, a cataloguer of the physical world, a philosopher regards the earth akin to how the elderly view meteorological science: they aren't sure it exists at all, and would prefer to have conversations about the weather, to know if *your* weather is *their* weather.

A geologist is unlike the poet, who bobs in an ocean of anticipatory nostalgia for the physical world despite paying taxes within it, her body darting around like a little lost bird heart, fast and meaty. And the geologist is unlike the prostitute, who becomes unto herself a heroic virtuoso of the physical. A made-to-order thumb harp.

The discovery of an ancient animal skeleton can make a person feel suddenly proud in a parental kind of way, like an astronomer who names a star for his daughter and sees it as homage rather than absurd, if poignant, sentimentalism. It was William who discovered the first nonavian dinosaur, the "Great Fossil Lizard," or Megolasaurus. He intended to announce his discovery in a publication in 1822 but it failed to print, and so for some time the dinosaur had what is called in science a *nomen nudum,* a naked name, given to an organism when the circumstances of discovery and its given name haven't yet been published in print. In other words, the Megolasaurus was baptized but not yet confirmed.

Other scientists began talking about the bones himself, scooping William's discovery, so there was a race to name the thing like the race to the moon, or a race to *name* the moon—which seems a good metaphor for naming a dinosaur which is, after all, another terrifyingly large thing humans had never seen up close. One scientist named Ferdinand tried to christen the Great Lizard with a complete binomial: *megalosaurus conybeare.* That one is *nomen oblitum*—a name to be forgotten, as scientists didn't much take to it.

The name is not supposed to be used. I apologize. Please forget the forgotten name and remember only the thing it is called today, a name given in 1827: *Megolasaurus bucklandii.* I offer you this anecdote by way of penance: when I was a girl, I went to a Christian summer camp called Camp Tecumseh located near Delphi, Indiana, on the Tippecanoe River. The girls in my cabin and I moved through woods to make it to chapel on Sundays, rows of wood benches set into a hillside by the lake, in front of a giant wooden cross. While there, I made everyone call me Charlie. Charlie was a good sport. Charlie prayed nightly and woke at dawn to swim. Because of Camp Tecumseh, Margaret Atwood's "Death by Landscape" has always haunted me: the reluctant, small landscape paintings in the narrator's living room, the girl dropping from the cliff silent as Wordsworth's Lucy Gray disappearing— poof!—into a puff of snow while crossing a river. Girl vanishings are very quiet. *Nomen oblitum.*

My parents were engaged after one week of dates. On the first, my father got a flat tire and exited the car in the Indiana heat, kicked the hubcap, and cursed. Still they made it to open mic night at a local bar where my father sang a Dylan song in his sly baritone and watched as my mother chatted with a man to her left. When answering his question about how his performance went, my mother said something affirmative, to which my father asked, pointedly, *How do you know.* My mother felt this irritability, quickness to anger, jealousy made him legible. He was not, as she would later tell it, *a game player. He is,* she would say with equal parts resignation and self-congratulation, *what he is,* by which she meant recognizable, totemic, and static as asphalt.

When they married, my mother erased her middle name, which had been her mother's name, Marie, to make space for her maiden name. She traded her mother's name to ensure her father's would stay, on documents and such. My mother's father had died of a stroke when she was nineteen. He was working in the pharmacy he ran when a strong headache suddenly came on. Excusing himself, this man—Charles, a man I never met, who one could say was grandfather in name only—walked into his office, pausing to pick up the *Encyclopedia Brittanica* which he had been reading in fits and starts that year. Surrounded by white porcelain jars full of gelatin capsules, powders of various granulation, and apothecary jars scrawled with gold enamel script, the tall man wearing glasses dropped to the floor. The man who liked science and played the trumpet in his spare time.

Portraits show William wearing a large blue pouch off his hip, hung jauntily from a belt loop. Reportedly it held mammoth teeth, skin, fossilized dung, and a hyena skull. One painting in Westminster Abbey shows him holding the skull: he wears a large dark robe and smiles, looking out at something to the right. The background is black. He cradles the skull, his round pink face floating happily in the darkness.

William used to race down the aisles of his lecture hall dressed like a Franciscan preacher, shoving the hyena skull in the faces of terrified undergraduates. He would shout repeatedly "What rules the world?" One student replied "Haven't an idea," to which William replied "The stomach, sir, rules the world. The great ones eat the less, the less the lesser still!"

I have never held an animal skull that I can offhand recall, though it seems a thing I've likely done. My brother and I once got lost in the Hoosier National Forest after smoking some pot and feared we'd not make it out by night. The sky darkened like an invitation that opens to reveal a dark gold sheen. The fall leaves were in some places nearly up to our knees, as though we were wading through a burning lake. Eventually I was delighted to find one small deer antler for my trouble. Today I display it on my fireplace mantle, where it sprouts like a fat hard branch from a vase of the same color. Occasionally my son takes it and jabs it menacingly at his sister.

After his neighbors stumbled on some unusually large bones, William began a dig in a limestone cave in south Wales in 1823. Besides a mammoth skull were pieces of a human skeleton that had been wrapped in fabric dyed with red ochre, a pigment derived from wet iron oxide and which varies according to local soil. Where a pocket might have once been was a handful of periwinkle shells; around the waist, a belt of small rods made of mammoth bone. Around its neck was a strand of perforated seashells.

It was as though the red bones had hummed there under the earth like matchsticks waiting to be lit. William was sure, along with other Reverends then and now, that before Noah's flood there was—at least as far as humanity is concerned—nothingness. This belief, alongside the jewelry, led William to declare he'd uncovered the burial site of a Roman prostitute or witch. The latter seemed most likely because a sheep's shoulder blade, which was once thought to have magical powers, was buried with the body. The body was also, he later wrote, thin and tall, "as a witch should be." Roman prostitutes used to dip lead-coated combs in vinegar, carrying them through their hair so the salts would deepen their color. How heavy that must be. Heavy as a whalebone corset, chastity belt, as the discovery of one of the world's oldest ceremonial burials.

The skeleton shifted shape many more times in William's mind. She ran a gambler's casino out of her sorceress's cave, was a witch, a tax collector. She may have even been Eve herself, William quipped, which would explain her red color: "for it is not extraordinary when Adam was made of [red earth], that his rib should have a tinge of ruddle."

He named her the Red Lady of Paviland.

Red ochre is a pigment found in Tuscan clay. Its painstaking procurement is described by the fifteenth century Italian painter Cennino Cennini, who, having hunted and dug for it in the mountains, says it runs through the land *like a scar on a face*. He used it to paint flesh, buildings, draperies. It's easier to excavate metal from the earth and grind it into pigment— *you actually cannot grind too much,* Cennini says— than to excavate a skeleton and shape it into a story, especially without eradicating evidence which is, as we know by now, another word for history.

Once I overheard a docent at the Chicago MOMA explain to children how x-rays revealed Picasso's *Old Man with a Guitar* was painted onto a canvas originally painted with the figure of a woman. One could, she explained, just barely make out the woman's hip with the naked eye. Though the paint making out her hip is literally under the old man's leg, in a certain light it appears she is sitting on his lap. In her talk the docent uncovered two things at once: the woman beneath, and, as such, the ironic impossibility of the man's loneliness. The painting was begun during his Blue Period, so it's likely the woman was a prostitute; during this time Picasso painted prostitutes, beggars, and drunks in varied shades of blue, sinking into a depression worsened by the fact that no one wanted to buy his paintings of sad and poor people, leaving him, tautologically, poorer and sadder.

When analyzing the sketches of large game found in ancient cave systems, scholars have determined that some scrapes and dents in the stone surface indicates that the paintings were attacked, possibly *in the belief that harming the image would wound a real-life animal.* Thinking about this is like thinking about the holes in Francis Bacon's paintings, which can never be entered, and that is all right because they are terrifying.

When I was in middle school all the girls wore Wet n' Wild 501 lipstick. It was the color of a dangerous bruise, and like this we signaled we were not whores but witches.

In the 1950s some lab tech, assisted by carbon dating technology, read the Red Lady of Paviland's bone protein like a primer and found it was 20% fish, part woolly rhinoceros, part reindeer, and all male— not a Red Lady at all. For this error, perhaps Buckland should be forgiven. He became confused: the bones had been dyed in red ochre. They looked to him like food, like something to consume.

The *Oxford English Dictionary* gives three meanings to the word *consume.* A) adjective: of a foodstuff: suitable for consumption, edible. B) able to be destroyed, esp. by fire; combustible. C) noun: a commodity that is intended to be used up or worn out by use.

My son makes sense of death like this: the body of a person is chewed by animals or swallowed into a shallow belly of earth, so that, in being consumed, one becomes and becomes and becomes, always becoming. Never dissolved. At night his body becomes very hot, his feet twitch, and he explains to me how, in death, he will fold up inside a scarlet macaw and we will meet somehow in our new jungle.

Let us imagine that, while William carried the Red Lady from the cave like a new, clackity bride, his living wife— Mrs. Buckland—Mary, neé Morland—offered their sons a geography lesson using globes she had made by hand out of colored paper, and inflated. Mary was a scientist but her husband disapproved. Her son later said she was "particularly clever and neat in mending broken fossils," and many of these reconstructions are now preserved at the Oxford University Museum of Natural History under the name *Buckland*.

For his part William became more skilled, learned there is an art to digging, that there are delicate excavations and excavations akin to lobbing a porcelain dish at a wall. He learned that there was much before the flood. He became, in fact, author of *Evidence of the Flood*, in which he pointed out it is irrelevant whether one calls it a flood or a glacier. The water simply wiped out everything before.

So much anxiety over water, ice; the female body, the belief that it speaks only in symbols, meaning, it speaks without argument, is simply made of ovaries, periwinkle, spit, antiquity. In this way the female body is like the *afikomen* hidden in the house during the seder: present yet undiscovered. Fragile yet foundational. Most consumable when consumptive. Most ideally, a delicious unknown.

When people describe having always felt one sex or another, assigned or not, or, for that matter, attraction to one sex or another, straight or not, I feel disappointed. The rhetoric of sustained identity is the cause of so much trouble. Doesn't human desire shift as dispassionately, as organically, as land? Maybe their insistence on a fixed identity is because what they really love is to unearth—to pry something— a lie, an infidelity, an inconsistency— out of someone. To excavate a hidden identity—the meat of a walnut from its enamel-like shell, the rib from its cavernous cathedral—a delicate, fantastical process.

I am failing to be clear. I feel like an engine that won't turn over. I carry the knowledge of my history like a carapace.

Sometimes a scholar names a thing, and it falls under the waves of time and is worn smooth like a stone until it no longer appears a discovery. Then a new scholar names the same original thing and it is suddenly new again, like an excavation of discourse. In archeological excavation there is a similar existential vertigo—discovery stretching one's imagination over tens of thousands of years. It is strangely reassuring, if you tend to tire of yourself and your contemporaries.

If a thing was buried long ago, it may now need a new burial, a more modern to-do. The Red Lady's bones are now a museum display. The curators have arranged them on a glass table, and a projector shines down like the sun, projecting the outline of form, of flesh. In this exhibit the Red Lady has been transformed from waiting-to-be-discovered to a patchwork skeleton worth celebrating, a vintage diva, a reality show winner. I think of Snow White, or a crime outline, or Alexander McQueen's best work except she is 30,000 years old and the Real Thing with real bones, not a dummy wearing a gown that looks like a bird or a fire or wet iron oxide or— irony—a skeleton.

Gentlepersons, the Red Lady of Paviland, the first human fossil found in what appears to be the oldest ceremonial burial in all of western Europe—the tinny voice chimes eternally from the speaker, inviting intentional mishearing: *gentle purse on. Thread laid Eve… the first hue man…*

Afikomen: a word originating with the Greek *epikomen*, meaning "that which comes after."

In his sixteenth century anatomy treatise *De Humani Corporis Fabrica,* Vesalius draws his dissected bodies standing, feet planted firmly in fields, the city off in the distance. Flayed from top to bottom, dead, and inaccurate, the faces are somehow triumphant—this one, a superhero lobbing his discus at the sun.

Recently I began to paint. I bought tubes of acrylic paints from the Michaels in town. I bought a used easel and a drafting table that stood in the corner of the office unused and discerning. I painted women's faces, very large and very fast, as a child learning guitar bangs out chords. I found pictures of women everywhere; on book covers, in bookstores, magazines. I gave them green faces. Then one day a friend visited and I showed her the paintings, both sheepish and proud. *You have always painted,* she told me. I didn't recall. *Before you left Missouri, you gave me a painting of a vase of flowers.* I didn't recall. *It is still hanging in my house,* she said. I said, *Well! What do you know. Here are some sad looking women.*

I have not brought these threads together. I've been an inefficient spider, an engine that won't turn over. I have made for you, as I wished, a museum of the Red Lady.

Sometimes I pretend to be William and he speaks like a professor: *I, like all men of science, know the body because of women and criminals; it was the dissection of these that founded modern medicine and gave us the ecstatic illustrations in De Humani Corporis Fabrica.*

After the flood Noah sent out a raven and a dove into the wildness. The raven circled, it is said, until the water was dry. The dove was sent for confirmation that the water had receded. For centuries religious scholars have puzzled over the symbolism and most especially, the sequence. Why the raven first? Some say raven means death, dove means peace. Raven may mean storms, or deliciousness, or the child's delight in destruction. Dove may mean storms, or deliciousness, or the child's delight in destruction. Wildness may mean that which is untouched by civilization, by humanity; that which is estimable only by other animals.

Sometimes I pretend to be William and he speaks like a lover: *my love, my red love, my Achilles of petticoats.* I listen to myself-as-William and throw up my hands in ecstasy at the unknowing, the elegant misnomers, until William and I become the dove, the raven, the water: all of it, returning home to Ararat.

Notes

"The First Deluge: A Found Poem" and "Mrs. Noah: A Found Poem": the text of each of these poems was excerpted and has been very slightly edited and rearranged from the website www. christiananswers.net.

"The Great Disappointment": Rev. William Miller predicted the Rapture in 1843 using a system of calculating days from the Bible that he devised. Thousands were convinced two separate times that the day would come. When each passed, they and Miller became the subject of public ridicule. It came to be known as "the great disappointment." The story of the girl who brought a trunk full of her dresses for the Rapture is told in John Greenleaf Whittier's account of Millerism. See "The World's End," in *Tales and Sketches of The Works of John Greenleaf Whittier*, Vol. 5.

"The Book of Revelation": There are references throughout this poem to the Book of Revelation as translated in the standard King James Version of the New Testament.

In that poem the lines "an island is part of the earth" is taken from Margaret Wise Brown's exemplary children's book *The Little Island;* this book is also referenced in "Boats in the Attic" ("the kitten / trying to learn faith / from the island")

'Missing File #1: Woolly Rhinoceros / Ancient Cavity Tooth":

Paul Pettit, Paul Bahn, and Sergio Ripoll, eds., *Palaeolithic Cave Art at Creswell Crags in European Context* (London: Oxford University Press, 2007).

Andy Heil, "Siberia Surrenders Woolly Rhino Mysteries," December 6, 2012, www.rferl.org/a/russia-zoology-wolly-rhinoceros-boesk orov/24791250. Accessed June 5, 2020.

"Missing File #3: Panthera Leo Leo, Or, A Civics Lesson":

Aristotle, *History of Animals in Ten Books* (London. H. G. Bohn, 1862).

"Missing File #4: Already We Are Less than Before":

"Larry King Interviews Transhumanist FM-2030," www.youtube.com/watch?v=XkMVzEft7Og. Accessed June 7, 2020.

William Wordsworth, *The Prelude: 1799, 1805, 1850*, ed. Jonathan Wordsworth, M. H. Abrams, and Stephen Gill. (New York: Norton Critical Editions, 1979).

John Clare, *The Progress of Rhyme*. In John Clare, *Major Works*, ed. Eric Robinson and David Paulin (Oxford: Oxford University Press, 1984).

"Missing File #5: The Ortolan Bunting": the ortolan is a tiny and rare bird long considered the "songbird of France." In gastronomy, it is force-fed by being placed in a dark box with millet. As a reaction to darkness it eats continuously; it is often then drowned alive in brandy. Gourmands cover their heads and face with a large napkin or towel in order to absorb the aroma as they consume the entire bird at once; they also do so, legend has it, to protect their identity from the wrath of God (this ritualistic use of the towel was begun by a priest). It is illegal in France to cook and eat the ortolan, though several chefs are petitioning for holidays from the law.

The author would like to thank the following friends and writers who helped shape this book: Maggie Smith, Elizabeth Frost, Kit Frick, Jessica Garratt, Mary Speaker, Katie Hartsock, Susan McCarty, Marcela Sulak, and Julia Choffel. The writing was made possible by attendance at several artist colonies, each supported by Oakland University: Virginia Center for the Creative Arts and Moulin de Nef, the Rockvale Writer's Colony, and the Crosshatch Center for Arts and Ecology.

I must also thank dear friends Joanie Lipson Freed, Rachel Gurstein, Liz Shesko, Emily Raabe, Alix Olson, Julie Lambert, and Jessica Garratt in particular, as well as my family, Frona, Ron, Aaron, and Liz Powell, and my aunt Grace Hamilton. I am grateful to my son, Samuel, whose brilliance and determination is woven throughout the book. My daughter, Anita, provided buoyancy and grace as I navigated the writing of these poems. Finally, I owe more thanks to my partner, Alex, than I can say here.

Acknowledgments

I am grateful to these journals for publishing the following, often in earlier versions:

A Public Space, "Missing File #1: Woolly Rhinoceros / Ancient Cavity Tooth"

American Literary Review, "Conditions"

Alaska Quarterly Review, from "The Book of Revelation" (as "The Book of Revelations") ("Someone has given your mother")

Black Warrior Review, "Missing File #5: The Ortolan Bunting," "Missing File #6: Horns-a-Plenty"

Copper Nickel, "Etymology: Heaven"

Crazyhorse, "After the Birth of the First Child," "Boats in the Attic," from "The Book of Revelation" (as "The Sun Is a Star We Only See in the Daytime") ("One day in the car / my son says")

Cream City Review, "In the Beginning"

The Greensboro Review, from "The Book of Revelation" ("The first child arrived")

Hayden's Ferry Review, "If We Speak of the Hurricane" (republished on www.poets.org), "Nomen Nudum"

The Inquisitive Eater, "A Few Facts about Bees"

jubilat, "Upon Turning Forty"

Michigan Quarterly, "The Great Disappointment"

Prairie Schooner, "The First Deluge," from "The Book of Revelation" (as "The Book of Revelations") ("In the Book of Revelations / there is great equality of number")

Proximity Magazine, "Missing File #4: Already We Are Less than Ever Before"

Many of the "Missing File" pieces (numbers 1–5, 7) were originally published in a chapbook with Black Lawrence Press titled *The Art of Perpetuation* (2020).

Alison Powell is Associate Professor of English at Oakland University. Her other collections include a chapbook titled *The Art of Perpetuation* (Black Lawrence Press, 2020) and a collection of poetry titled *On the Desire to Levitate* (Ohio University Press, 2014). Her work has appeared in the *Boston Review*, *PBS NewsHour*, *poets.org*, *A Public Space*, and *Michigan Quarterly Review*, among others.

Gary Keenan

Rotary Devotion

Michael D. Snediker

The New York Editions

Gregory Mahrer

A Provisional Map of the Lost Continent

Nancy K. Pearson

The Whole by Contemplation of a Single Bone

Daneen Wardrop

Cyclorama

Terrence Chiusano

On Generation & Corruption

Sara Michas-Martin

Gray Matter

Peter Streckfus

Errings

Amy Sara Carroll

Fannie + Freddie: The Sentimentality of Post–9/11 Pornography

Janet Kaplan
The Glazier's Country

Robert Thomas
Door to Door

Julie Sheehan
Thaw

Jennifer Clarvoe
Invisible Tender

Lightning Source UK Ltd.
Milton Keynes UK
UKHW011506110822
407174UK00003B/949